DUMMY VENTRILOQUIST

MICHELLE BITTING
POEMS

C&R Press
Conscious & Responsible

DUMMY VENTRILOQUIST

TABLE OF CONTENTS

For You (prelude)

I.

II.

For You

I heard a song—

It was you, laughing.

A sound so

Beautiful

And more so being

Made

By your impossibly human

Body.

And flying out

Of it, the heart—

A winged red

Thing—looking

To save

And be saved.

I.

For Phil

All day we've bent
like Benedictine monks

over armoires and bookshelves,
rubbing the house clean

of grime and wicked thick
dust, pausing but once

to drop our robes and oil
each other bright as snakes

entwined in the grass
of our sun-bolted bed.

You never left me
or the strange world of my childhood

I carry like a mourner
on my back, never quite able

to set the black box down
and leave it behind

without turning back
to turn it around.

Three decades I've waited
to jump the suicide train

my family tracks like a runaway
beneath coastal starlight,

a southern cross
I note and bind in books

stretched from ghost smoke
like a cigarette

I wish I had
but I'm trying not to do that

because *I like my body*
when it's with your body—

two strands of the same
high-voltage cable

holding me damp and sparking
day or night against

the green skin of the dark.

Look At What Happens When Two Galaxies Collide
~Science section headline, *The Atlantic*, August 2022

Have you ever seen
two marching bands moving
toward each other? It can take
500 million years
for two bodies made of dust
to merge, forming a heart of
pink crests—two knees kissing
—seamless in the sky
as musicians gliding across
water. Like Mustang horses,
their wild engines tearing
down the cosmic
plain, slashing gravity
to art, trampling nebulous
grasses, the night's velvet barn
bust open. Love can do
some pretty astonishing
things, like make dead
matter come alive, the grave
turned gymnasium, tragedy
tuned humorous, the dagger
now a breast filling the paradise
cupboard where my glass
is found always full, water
seeding a curved universe,
blessing the four corners
of each light-spattered door.
I have no excuse
mistaking your eyes
for disco balls, stars
scattered down my front
like spilled coffee,

the hotter angles
of God's essence
nailed to me in radiance,
in arrows hustling the edges
of everything home.
There is no excuse
for the mystery love is, but
to the boy in sixth grade
who slipped his unsigned
valentine inside my desk
when I wasn't looking,
your invisible collapse
has not gone unnoticed—
the genius of its design
a black hole in time
where I hold hands with you
at the heat of it
that is neither silence
nor nothingness but
the hidden mess
of a million suns.

Everyday Ablutions
~after Saj Issa's "Ablution of Faith and Frustration"
      (ceramic on wood, 2020)

This garment called life,
ill-fitted for so long, falls
away. I am sky—naked—
and a human enterprise
with three days rain
writing truth across my
face, spines of micro blue
lashing the horizon,
feeding a mountain's green

ear. Without remembering
why, I remove my shoes
and walk a cold geometry,
spinning my points, a noiseless
star pinned to a system
of bright tales—my revolving
fires. Timeless, I will travel
through, sins waving at
scars no longer called

foreign. How pure the broken-up
patterns—clouds that morph
and blur masses billowing
inside. I don't know why
it became impossible, this task
of faith. Only clearer now,
framed in relief like this
on a museum wall. What's
erased overcame me. And I have
to *bow not knowing to what.*

Yet, the Loveliness

Once, Dorianne told me
of the moment her mother finally
admitted, apologized even,
for the spotty passage
of her child-hood years, how often
they proved a woods rife with wolves
and teeth and trickery enough
to make a girl want to gaze into
the maw of an open oven
and mistake that boundless dark
for a candle. The loveliness I wanted
would have cost my mother
nothing—a thimble of breath, a wisp
of floss the sparrow plucks
from the gutter and threads
into her egg chamber behind
my front porch lamp—or,
the last thumb of indigo milk
tugged from breast before
my mother crunched those lovelies
beyond the borders of her garments,
their nickel hooks and eyes,
her secret queendom—
a language of the body
she was not taught to teach
or promote. Oh fragile basket
we swing through thickets
of time, combing the thorns
for brighter berries
we can crush against our chests
like medals or gauze,
staunching the grief, our yearn
for honesty—for a true line
on the tongue—
how sweet the taste of even one.

A Weird Science

Started at twelve and kept growing inside me like Marie Curie's matter—radioactive glow of my bones, electric eye pulsing atop my dime store microscope, the protozoa dolls an animated voodoo out of nowhere, pill-shaped specters that shimmied across cut glass slides, ghost worms I'd grown from hay & water cribs of my mother's leftover mason jelly jars. I laid them down along a garage of obscure edges where I've fled my whole life to perform experiments in not dying. Magic from the hand, from pots & pans and not *what teacher said to do makin' dreams come true*. But what else is there except go a little nuclear when it's 1972 and you're sent to school with a box of Re-Elect Nixon pens for passing out to white Anglo-Saxon friends? Some man's agenda Frankenstein-ed into us— domination seeds slipped between our unsuspecting teeth until the heart hungers for shadow metals that will burn a wielding wrist but do the trick reflecting truth. I sweated over it like Marie in her Victorian collars hunched over Petri, her tubes & beakers & burettes conjuring mass from marrow that could multiply, worms & grasses I fumbled with in the dark of my home-made lab. And why not? If when not there, we split axioms & hairs at school, us elementary girls ignited to break uniform chains like the skirts we couldn't hike past knee? You know, in case rangy males preyed ferally, the bulbs of their mouths & eyes popped wide by thigh skin. Which is exactly what happened when the plots cooked up behind stalls of the break-time bathroom materialized. Should you seek a method, our science came down to this: on the count of three, the clock clicked twelve and we dropped our lunches, rose through funk & steam of bananas & baloney sandwiches to rush the osculating windows—with our hands, unfastened them—fleeing the shocked mugs of boys & men left speechless in the room. We hurled our bodies to banks of overgrown ivy below, a safe & sexy mattress. Kush of stems & snails we crunched & buoyed up from, sailing free, mutating in that instant, poison a power & contagion of the vein hitting us and the ground running. We were bolted to air and a radiance of green. We let it blow us wild to the future, reins in teeth, our noble fire no one dared chase. Or dared contain.

Let Kids Be Kids
~after Frank O'Hara

I don't know what you're up to, America
But what I do know
It's not good for the body
Children need fresh air
An Ave Maria over their flesh
Their choice of friends
The theater of their identity
That is so complex
No single man from Florida
(The real sinner here)
Can decide—
If you ask me
What are you up to, America?
Criticizing how souls
Dress on a Saturday
Who they are
Who they hold hands
Or play hooky with
In movie theaters
No one needs the Hail Mary
Of running to far-away streets
Preyed on by gods know what
Mothers, you are glamorous countries
It costs you everything
Not to keep the peace
Not to keep hate
From taking the hearts of
Humans you love
Wasn't your first sexual experience
A blessed box of chocolates
Stirred into gratuitous barrels of buttered popcorn?
And if it wasn't I am sorry

MICHELLE BITTING

Oh Mothers
There are many bridges
Between heaven and earth
Built of strange and wonderful colors
Only the empty
The greedy for gravy on TV
(A dark growth campaigning on the innocent)
(It's unforgivable the latter)
Can't see them
Mothers (and I mean Fathers, Sisters, Brothers,
Grandfathers, Uncles, Cousins, Aunts, Grandmothers,
Friends and the entire United State
Of Nurturing Tolerance)
You don't want your tykes
Hanging around their rooms
Broken in your yards
There is no joy in that particular darkness
Who is to blame?
If you don't take this advice
And they're no longer here
Only embossed silver people
The images in photographs
You talk to when you're old
Because you wouldn't let them be
Wouldn't let them love
Who they were when they were young

Now at Holiday Time I Think About the Moment I Heard You'd Passed On
~Joan Didion (December 5, 1934 – December 23, 2021)

How I felt a cold shadow creak through me—klieg
lights suddenly flipped, a few mercury vapors streaking
noir effects, growing up in L.A. where I'd read
you, run into you at the tucked-away girls' school
your daughter attended, a stone's throw from lots
where talented Sharon Tate expired and Jim Morrison
fluttered psychedelic, fiery birds rising from the boulevard
of broken wings. Sometimes the calendar opens too early,
the advent candy, its hidden splendor, spoiling like
chocolate in the sun of disbelief, our soft mugs stamped
with bad news behind each sprung paper door parceled
down a page, each bittersweet morsel we've fed ourselves
to live, the un-swaddled mirror swallowed—darkly—
embraced. Each death, like yours, we're summoned to face.

A Touch of Evil

If you want a happy ending, that depends, of course, on where you stop your story. ~Orson Welles

Why pretend its wicked fingertip hadn't already found me that summer I was twelve and friendless between schools, lost in my awkward body and psyche—a war of worlds waged by gland and raging corpuscles running dialogue between my legs and brain's jejune tragedies—and why not join the community theater, young talent aspiring to be seen, wannabes signed on as juvenile background for the ersatz San Juan Hill street scenes of *West Side Story* even though, like the famous opening tracking shot in Orson Welles' late noir gem that goes on and on without edit, from the close up of a ticking bomb tucked into the trunk of a '56 Chrysler convertible to the moment three minutes later when the newlyweds kiss and the car goes up in flames just beyond a border checkpoint, even though that was filmed in Venice, California near the beach and not in a Mexican town called Los Robles out of which Chuck Heston emerges with faux black mustache, metal badge, bad accent, and last name Vargas—it's all a matter of illusion and suppression of people dying to be in America, and I, too, am an imposter from the west side of Los Angeles and while I may be green I know what it is to both bully and be bullied—the spiteful inner derangement that comes from that, so I figure I'll spend the summer where no one knows me and try to find a self while ogling grown up actors who keep falling in and out of love, and in and out of bed with each other from what I can gather at my invisible edge of the commissary cart and overheated wings of Barnum Hall where the hopeful neophytes gather to swoon and hiss at each other like bust open fire hydrants in a mid-city heat wave, that is, when they're not called to kick a leg up or empty their lungs of song on cue under the hot stage lights as the sun grows long in tooth only to get yanked at the end of doggie August which is the nature of love I'm gathering while doing my best to not fall off a labyrinth of catwalks and rails I've been assigned to clamber and scale like a gangly little bug alongside union grips and gaffers as I am but a casting dot in the play's human scenery and so not called much to rehearse, but Michael the master fly man who makes the scenery soar and takes his job very seriously while also maybe being a bad boy I'm thinking—I'm not sure but all those guys have tons of tats and pull up to the parking lot mornings a little worse for wear—red eyes, leathers and Harleys and no one will dispute the theater is a dangerous place with its web of intricate beams in the wizard dome overhead but out of sight where the magic strings get pulled, where suddenly the backdrop of a high school dance turns dress shop interior or vertiginous maze of windows, bricks, and fire escapes thanks to the perfectly balanced system of ropes, C-clamps and pygmy weights, the dangling lanterns that weigh fifty pounds and will take your head off if they fall on you, but Mike whose eyes match the butterfly blue of the So Cal sea on a Venice postcard, ocean I grew up in and also there's his wicked grin and billowing brown locks and a mustache that's a bit like Chuck Heston's in the flick I mentioned about murder and mayhem which is how my insides feel most of the time and maybe Mike senses this and knows what I need is some controlled burn, so to speak, a taste of managed danger so I can better relate to the ticking clock inside so it doesn't detonate all at once or until I say because I'm controlling this shot and I'm the director of me and I can stretch this out and continue to show up every day in my cheap, ill-fitting bell bottoms and dumb floral tees from JC Penney's, ready to climb higher and higher and one-handed even, yes, I am clutching each rung for dear life under my sweaty pubescent armpits because they've tasked me with ferrying sustenance to the gaffers in the gallery—caddies of coffee and donuts from Winchell's, all the way up through the ropes and cables, the battens and pipes, the mid-travelers and fire curtain, up, up, through the hellish swelter and motes that make me sneeze and I have to stop and catch my breath sometimes and not look down or think about the rats in the massive Deco walls so that when I reach the top and give over the doughy and liquid goods, all I can do is roll my shaking fetal self onto the grid deck

MICHELLE BITTING

and fly tower summit, dizzy and more alive than ever like I just grew a few inches or years and Mike has a look of the devil about him, I mean, if my parents could see me they'd have him arrested for child endangerment I'm pretty sure but I don't care because I've let that girl go—dropped her down to doll, to dust, to ant on the boards a hundred feet below, and I'm gasping a little when I hand Mike his Styrofoam of brew and sticky maple twist, and when he peels the plastic white lid away and peers across the steam, sipping, his blue eyes slice through me and I know I've done something holy—I could be in heaven—and then his head ticks to one side like a timer and his smile clicks into place and the silence around us explodes when he says: *You made it, Kid, and look at that—coffee's not just hot, it's on fire.*

The Great Fire

In the forest of my mind, I like to imagine
skins of Giant Sequoias thick enough to endure
a rapidly heating planet. The way the ceilings of London's
Old Globe maintained their thatched oak shape even
after The Great Fire. Theater being the haven we leap
toward to both rekindle and escape what burns
us humanly up, sniffing sulphur from our seats. When
plague grips a grand city in its pitch and airless fist,
flames bore holes in flesh that the rats sing sweetly
through. Music being both solvent and lifeline, hauling
us out when longing dissolves every part we think to toss
in. Sometimes I light myself on fire and watch small
bodies skitter my edges. Buildings I'm
constructing from each scalded shadow fled.

An Exercise in Love
~after Diane di Prima

I was remembering with Gail
over coffee in Topanga how
I used to choke up thinking
about my son's transition—about
the dresses of many colors
no longer needed we'd slipped
like pretty fish from their wires
inside his closet's unlit shell
and floated to a thrifty coastal store.
I suppose there are moments
together, inhaling a favorite
indie film or albacore rolls
at an L.A. eatery,
when I've caught the eyes
of strangers squinting at him
from behind their pebbly
centerpieces, like stunned sea
anemones when the sun pokes
a socket of clouds
and muscles them open, blessing
a son's sacred face that is pure
moonstones and cherubs and
green hills and heron feathers,
little sea grass tufts woven
on the ridge of his chin's
pocked shore due to regular
hormone injections.
I suddenly understand how
confused we all are, how utterly
wrong we've gotten it thus far,
us dinosaurs, us old barges, backwards
in our dreams of absolute

gender and pleasure.
Gail nods across the altar
of our canyon table and I follow
her eyes as I lift a toasted slice
to my lips, seeded with pomegranate,
sigh a cool scarf of breath
into my cup's hot shade. She
understands. My son I love
is just Emmet, gifting us *truth*
& *all-knowing* in Hebrew, *wholly*
universal in a distant German
tongue though my mouth
is saying just *Emmet*, over
and over, *Emmet—the smell*
of his hair, weaving the wind
the color of dawn: Emmet—
entirely himself, his name, his own.

Good Friday Ukraine Egg Verse

Yesterday, a crow rinsed its rare scrap of carrion in our backyard bath, mucking the waters, corpsing the flower bed with discarded entrails of some conquered creature—caught and scattered across the field. I like to imagine strangers, and good friends, too—gathered pagans and pilgrims, both, inside candle bright naves of churches or the every-day alters of living room tables blessed with brushes, beeswax, dank red and opaque dyes portending majesty and death, the tempered-in pastels of fairy tales we cloak horror in so children can sleep. Safika says when the sun's gone dark & gods disappear behind ink-blotted scenarios of sky, we follow the birds, as we always have, flying closer to the source, the raw yolk force of solar sorcery frowning down on grave slaughters of women, innocents, the lone man martyred on the skull bald head of Golgotha. I like to think of buried things—tender necks sprouting from severed bulbs, the eggs interred Safika says make cattle stronger and beehives lush with golden honey. Pysanka placed in a child's coffin so there's something to play with. Safika says eggs scribed with signs of living and the dead tunneled into ruins of their mothered earth promise return: a sprung and bloodied art, the human canvas of rebirth.

Pandemic Mask Sonnet

~with Wordsworth, Hayes, Millay

Nuns don't fret and nuns can be like children—
Good at caring less than politicians
About having to wear linen cages, separating
Viruses and life, *the song of the bird*
From the bone. The world's gone mad at *the wheel*
While bees and seas *soar for bloom*, germs and chaos
Straining against reorder. Confess the shape
Of your arrogance. So. Money. So amorphous, watching
From the bleachers. Our awful servitude, says
Youth: Don't panic! This fabric, this scanty plot
Of ground our mouths' dark box wrestles through words
For release can strike stars—*a little room set aflame.*
The prison unto which you've doomed our voice no prison is:
Love must be enough. Only that can't be destroyed.

There was, at last, the finding of the center...

Flood tide of ill fortune rising, we spent our days skirting the edge, bent backs gripped in the single seater as we leaned in to keep the cart from tipping. There's no knowing the speed to be gained, the steepness or drops, how wheels can fly off any second like shingles from a roof when the wind kicks up. Or the gradual sheering of tread until one day, metal plinks through matter like coins ripping a watery veil, tossed to the fountain floor. Suddenly, a whole family sunk, side-eyed silhouettes staring up from the mossy bottom, green flecks inhabiting our cheeks' scraped copper. It can feel like a fist smashed down, anvil cracking shapes in half like that crazed husband at an L.A. party who bashed his bald knuckles through the host's dead mother's dinette, crushing it like The Hulk, convinced this host had fucked his toney wife on the sly. True or not, the night wholly ruined. The guests stunned and helpless nibbling their meatballs made tangy by splintered glass and a ghost mom moaning in the vents. It can feel like presidents, shaved realities and razors reckoning. Fate, a fearsome judge—farm mistress with enough biscuits in her apron to satisfy the herd before they ride off and hogtie the hopeful horizon. Eventually hanging for it. Eventually the whip falling and throne split, smack down the middle where you need to be strongest, where the songbird flies from— free—if it's meant to sing.

II.

The Procession
~London, September 19, 2022

Makes its way from Buckingham to Westminster. Nothing
will halt the solemn coffin, the queen's straight shoot,
her carriage cloaked in Royal Standard: crimson-gold
crowned by a hive of diamonds abuzz its velvet throne.
Nothing to topple the stone facade of family, the princely
troops, epauletted guards in bearskin hats and lockstep
with military who wear their chests on their hearts in rows
of colorful plots. Big Ben tolls, baffled birds cease flight, an
echoing boom of guns shatters a muzzled sky. Even the mournful
masses flogging their grief in bundled flags doesn't break
this patterned spell, this ordered hype. Except for the one
wild creature harnessed to his team up front and center
who keeps tossing his head, nipping his neighbor,
slapping the air with his dark bristled mane, refusing
to mind the taut reins of a master. Horse unimpressed with
the one direction of it all, tethered like this to a map stretching
from a place he's already been to where they think he's going.

Reporting Back

When the men and women became
bully monsters
backed by scum
bent to fetch
golf balls off the green
& rolling in ink
from the slough.
When few
read print anymore, scrolling
the nets
& threatening to take it all,
including your baby's milk
bottle & last biscuit,
we thought
the headless horsemen riding
our direction
less terrifying.
Who says decapitation
is all bad, anyway?
Those free-floating cabezas—
ancient, adrift
on song-strung shores
are always ready to party.
Their salvaged seas,
their mystical gowns
sewn with so much to teach
about disruption.
The merit of dreams
hauled back from.
We should have drowned
this time. We should
be married
to air. In love

MICHELLE BITTING

with mystery
& fish, the hero-ed
dark, the matches
struck to keep
multitudes fed. The heart
swilled inside
the surfing eye
& risen lining,
the tides
we keep climbing
up the belly of the whale.

Your heart will forever break at what you are hearing

And when they bombed other people's houses, we protested but not enough... ~ Ilya Kaminsky

Dumbly, as the dregs at the bottom of a coffee cup. Wildly, like the light in my son's eyes after he cooks something hardy. I grow old and imagine taking a match to the barn, the roof and windowsills sweating more paint than scales in an aquarium. The house is a sponge with termites nestled in holes. Scary uniformed men poured poison in so now we sense the beams better. *Shut it*, the poet says. Your heart doesn't stop at what you hear. Not really. Termites, a certain breed. Subterranean but also winged. When the kids were small everything felt simple and exhausting at the same time. Beauty never got old. No one slept and my heart never broke, not really. My love's hearing goes but his blood is sweeter. Mine, bitter and bolted to earth. Beauty will be broken with all the vowels still intact. My heart might die. Your alphabet is older. I'll just shut it now. Let the dead kidnap my mouth.

In the Museum of the Dream Where I Am Falling from the Sky
~after Auden

And waking, realize I've gotten my suffering all wrong.
But startled, feel miraculous, mastering flight somehow.
A superhero three hundred feet up like that martyred son
eating sunbeams and treetops. The clouds, my roller skates
at the edge of the world. I gaze down on peoples' heads,
familiar crowds from past lives I want desperately to avoid.
I worry in my feathered trusses about what they'll say if I'm
seen up close and human. Then my dream flings opens and vision
crashes. I land dead center of the group that is crossing a bridge,
but they turn leisurely from my disaster, my silent cry, my
melting failure. They could care less, and their indifference
stings in relief. I am among them, and my clothes are off,
my pale legs a delicate ship with do-it-yourself kegs
of anxiety and torture stowed in every visible pore. You may
have heard the splash and been amazed, me and my not-so
innocent behind scratching green water. More likely, though,
you, like the others, had somewhere to get to and sailed calmly on.

I Should Have Known

The way my brother went on about our mother's cough
it was his way of pretending to be tough—

deflecting his own demise, his numbered days on Earth. At most
seven, if my memory serves. The past. Yes, but never the cost

of what's severed in the present. My mother stirred eggs over a stove's
blue flame for my brother in the morning, then settled in to love

together his favorite flick about the team of misfit girls and brash coach who said
There's no crying in baseball! The spotless upholstery on our mother's plaid

couch crisscrossing with cooked yolks & toast & undigested food
blurring inside my brother who was smart and, at heart, so very good

but in that moment in a very bad way, turns out. Understand? I can't
begin, knowing how rust and mold can erode our most tender want

too often in secret, shadowed spaces—doubt, a dark ballet
of demons—their oily coins waltzing through the wallet

of a mind's rank folds—the hand that waves from afar but will prove unsafe
for the wrist hoisting a HELLO! but meaning GOODBYE! outside the café

where we sat laughing for the last time, talking life. When I pass by, years later,
I see him smiling at me, quietly plotting to end it all, sipping a glass of water.

Braided Fugue State #4 (The Mothering)

I've been here before, in the backseat
    Of a blue station wagon - or am I driving?

        At thirteen, our son reached the decision
        Not to go on.

Somewhere around the old parish grounds.
    My father's in the car though I cannot see him.

        I'm retiring, he said, and found
          a length of rope coiled in the garage.

The car won't budge. I'm on an impossibly steep hill. Strapped
in upside-down. A stuck roller coaster.

        Behind the house, our son stared at the slope.
        I said: *It's too severe and covered in ivy.*

Click, click, click of gears underneath. My body making a
90-degree angle between sky and ground.

        He wanted to make a ladder of the rope—use it to
        scale the insane green façade.

I'm paralyzed, can't breach the summit—a bug on a wall to be
swatted. The sheerest plummet. When he got to the top

        he stood, defiant, straight up. Fists and eyes
        raised— screaming into the blue.

MICHELLE BITTING

Crime of the Century

Barreling down a coastal road, Supertramp's
"Dreamer" takes over the radio, Roger Hodgeson's
fingers drilling the dash open. It's the sound of 40 years
ago and a red tide—swarms of slippery, stinking fish
washed up—goners, all of them, rotting in a hot Pacific
shimmer. And my brother is there with me at a lunar edge
of wet: full moon glint, sulfur whiff, stiff bodies like spilled
quivers of small, silvery arrows pointing every whack way
around us, their stilled eyes wide like sinking babies flopped
in sopping blankets of shore, schools of strewn clock guts,
a splayed and gritty spawning. My brother and I sing along,
our car stopped, listening from the highway, letting the night
and sea chaos carry us: *dreamer, you know you are a dreamer...*

and we're in sync, somehow, same words, same starry string
of plinked notes chiming in the night's outlined breath.
Crystalized. It was like this: our skins close and a mineral breeze
clouding eyes, blowing back salt-ashed hair, the just-detected
distant spiral jetties. We unbolted metal doors to barefoot skate
the sand berms down, feel a cold crack of waves slap toes.
Stoned on weed and much too high to maneuver our muddied
minds and feet inside whatever plots we were churning, Brother,
whatever in our youth we thought ourselves big enough
to handle, whatever tides and misdemeanors, no worse
than what your hand would steer our way—your demise,
suicide—that ancient refrain recorded: a shocking dream
that wakes in song, even now, the human and remains.

Poem For the Left Behind

Once I stood like an actor
in a nightmare except
I was awake
and nothing fell from my mouth
but silence, but wagging
shadow—the singed
tongues of my brothers
rolled out on gurneys,
their grave eyes
searching the house
for a line, for a life
and finding, too soon
only soil.

Poor Yorick

On the lip of descent into chaos, my spirit
yearns for halcyon hours,
a longing for daisies, for excavated
jest, for the brother who slung me
like a cross over his shoulders
walking home from school, past
parochial lawns and gnarled
oaks, their old man steeple arms, past
Witchy Witchy Wilson's house—
spinster lady with unkempt hair
we'd glimpse on occasion watering her pansies
with a droopy black hose, a broken-necked
swan regurgitating rivers
into the eyes of her violet blooms. Everyone
crossed the street to avoid contact,
in case she cast a spell
or tried to eat us—the irony being
that when she died
she wasn't found for weeks
and rumor had it and neighborhood kids tattled
how her cats had nibbled away
at the decomposing flesh, alone
in a cruel world that doesn't touch
or move you until the full dark duende
shovels your dankest soil up
and with it the skull you name *Brother*,
the one who went crazy
years after he piggy-backed you home
but a minute ago, wasn't it?
I can hear his tender laughter
and I can touch the clown suit
made of many-colored squares mother sewed
that he loved to wear on Halloween,

big enough for a 6ft. man—the pleated
blue and white gingham collar
with pinking-sheared edges
that flared and circled his neck like a quilted corona,
his smile belying the pit
of goblins buried in his gut—
an inexplicably princely
and decaying gorgeous core
where worms grow fat as little gods
orbiting the dirt, or
thrumming and laughing beneath
sidewalks, the rotten marks
and hard-won steps
of brothers and sisters,
(and every living fool
when you think of it)
who eventually comes to pass.

Talking Ophelia with My Students I Think About My First Boy

Because we know what the bard implied about youth and what lust does when left to unchain the body's boundaries, weaving a crown around two blooming heads drawing shades down to test their naked billowing—a *blasted ecstasy*. It's only natural in the hushed shade of an evening when parents step out to maybe linger with friends over wine and roasted poultry at Buffalo Wild Wings, say, relishing animal spirits alongside televised sports that sometimes bloody like tender flesh on public display. I never thought anything more would come from my fist raw encounter one coastal afternoon in a room that smelled and sounded like the sea rushing through us. The only shame after was mandated by the state of they who made me and judging hands at play today, posing as the glass o fashion and the mould of form. Convinced H meant to stay close 2 O forever, she let him take her in: water that meant a river of currents called fear flooding them after. When my parents found my diaphragm on the windowsill, they called me into a darkened room of wood and distressed leather to say *we know how boys talk*. The cup in my hand was an earthquake stamped with vintage pink roses I've worked decades to quell, conjuring it like a curse, learning how. The father is a ghost of the mother's silence wandering a dead past. My students get depressed, driven mad by stupidity, by stone skirts and branches that drag them under as they wave, refusing to drown.

Nocturne Sonnet

I can see you through the kitchen's steamed up
window but you can't see me here in the dark,
not my moon-sheened arms like Victorian candles
sparking when rats rustle the bushes, not the crickets
weaving ghost crowns about my head watching you
plunge your fists into a sink's rust dome, erasing
dregs, the headless crusts of fish, Brussels sprout
flecks & basil dip that studded each plate until you
made them shine again. When smoothed & patted
planets align like children in their KitchenAid rack,
the gloss of life cracks and dies even in its greening, even
as days tower gold and long and I hear *old winter's song*,
the *went away* of reddening hours, the stay of love, but most
of all, *my darling*, most of all, *when autumn leaves start to fall.*

MICHELLE BITTING

In My Great Grandmother's Grave, Channeling Holmes

Somewhere in the lots of Forest Lawn Cemetery
your ribs are disintegrating to inscrutable grey
dust. It's cold in your coffin of black shellac, our satin
carton, our airless island of no escape. The trees
keep weeping and we've got work to do. Houdini
with his winched pirouettes won't wriggle past these
terminal locks. Who puts keyholes in coffins, anyway?
I want to burgle the dead. You've got trick jewels and I know it.
But my eyes without light have no clue. I'm on a trail
and the crimes are green, bloody, lucrative. Manly,
mainly. On paper—lapidary when exhumed. The mined
shaft always shows. Glow, I wish I could, and have cooked
you something nice before you died. I don't know
your favorites, but I could guess, feed myself into boots
of hounds-tooth and imagine steamed puddings
(you were English) some tapas of braised tongue
with spiced aioli (a part of you, Spain) drips of absinthe
for dessert—our sleep of choice when the dream's too
live and I'm still here, under glass, tramping weeds
from upside-down, kicking dead sidewalks, the grass
you keep sighing under in my elementary mind.

Portrait of Myself as Watson, My Great Grandmother, Sherlock Holmes

Because the men keep going missing and we like to wear the pants. We look good in tweed and love a long smoke sorting things out before a dark fire. She's been dead seven decades but her ghost sense burns better than green oils I like to sample at the medical store on Lincoln. We ride in my car and when the upholstery sweats patchouli I know I'm time traveling for real. A particular aroma swooping me back to 1981 Sundays and stumbling down Telegraph, bleary from the evening's indulgences, in need of aspirin and eggs. Being a doctor, I'm licensed to mix it up and sometimes Holmes and I switch hats—my bowler for his deerstalker. We both know I'm the one addictively inclined. At the end of each case I say *Bring me the needle, Watson* and he follows my clue to swap parts, unbuckles our bag of flowered ampules, the smashed and simmered petals that will take me far, far away. Hey, I dreamed us here in the first place, dressed up and armed us to unfasten latches, my black box opened in hot pursuit of fiends, a legacy of crimes and love that keeps crashing historical pages, our collective field of casualties. Enough souls lost to want to trace why all's not right or quiet on my western front.

Dummy Ventriloquist

~after "Not I: Throwing Voices" exhibit, LACMA, 2021

Or a misalignment of voice and body.
Some folks get paid
not to let you in. While my lips
won't move having mastered the virus
speaking through hidden
identities. The artist
with various hats on inside a bubbly
tower reduced to marbles in the mouth.
It's a dimensional bridge
and I am crossing it.
Super woody sneeze
with lip zipped!
I smell leather and cowboy boots.
Red trim transmitting ire inside
a deep-seeded ear. My crying bust
of a child. You can fear it.
You can dead hare and a falcon in the niche.
I've got my fingers carved into pinewood
with gems around the neck—my
mannequin pedestal.
Ur, Mutter,
I am not your doll.
More like neighborhood devil
or court jester. Friendly box
with the sound of its own making.
Relax, we don't want
what you have, Pygmalion. If you cross
that line you won't be heard.
The museum guard has fallen asleep.
When I listen to my voice lately, it feels like
it belongs to the not me anymore.

ACKNOWLEDGEMENTS

Cleaver Magazine: "For Phil"

Catamaran: "Look At What Happens When Two Galaxies Collide"

The Nelligan Review: "Everyday Ablutions"; "A Touch of Evil"

Bear Review: "Yet, the Loveliness"

MockingHeart Review: "A Weird Science"; "Let Kids Be Kids"; "Poem for the Left Behind"

Vox Populi: "Now at Holiday Time I Think About the Moment I Heard You'd Passed On; "The Great Fire"; "Pandemic Mask Sonnet"; "In the Museum of the Dream Where I Am Falling from the Sky"; "Reporting Back"

Beat Not Beat California Anthology: "An Exercise in Love"

Cultural Daily: "Good Friday Ukraine Egg Verse"

Interlitq: "There was, at last, the finding of the center…"

The Night Heron Barks: "Your heart will forever break at what you are hearing"

The Banyan Review: "Braided Fugue State #4 (The Mothering)"

One: Jacar Press: "Talking Ophelia with My Students, I Think About My First Boy"

Psaltery & Lyre: "In My Great Grandmother's Grave, Channeling Holmes"

Los Angeles Review: "Portrait of Myself as Watson, My Great Grandmother, Sherlock Holmes"

Action, Spectacle: "Nocturne Sonnet"

SWWIM: "Crime of the Century"

Al-Khemia Poetica: "The Procession"; "I Should Have Known" (nominated for Best of the Net, 2023)

ONE ART: a journal of poetry: "Poor Yorick"

Air/Light: "Dummy Ventriloquist"

NOTES & GRATITUDE

"For Phil" riffs on lines by Joseph Millar and e.e. cummings.

Poem line and title from Oingo Boingo's "Weird Science."

"Let Kids be Kids" borrows language and voice from Frank O'Hara's "Ave Maria."

"A Touch of Evil" is my homage to the long tracking shot in Orson Welles' famous film noir of the same name.

The Great Fire of London broke out in 1666. It is considered the worst fire in London history and destroyed most of the civic buildings.

On February 24th, 2022, Russia invaded Ukraine in a major escalation of the Russo- Ukrainian war which began in 2014.

"The Procession" reflects on Queen Elizabeth's funeral, September 8th, 2022.

"In the Museum of the Dream Where I am Falling from the Sky" riffs on W. H. Auden's poem "Musée des Beaux Arts."

"Crime of the Century" is the title of a Supertramp album released in 1974.

"Nocturne Sonnet" includes phrases from the gorgeous 1945 song by Kosma and Prévert, eventually translated by Johnny Mercer.

"In My Great Grandmother's Grave…" and "Portrait of Myself as Watson…" imagine situations and dialogues with my great grandmother Beryl Mercer, actress.

"Dummy Ventriloquist" is an ekphrastic poem penned while walking around an exhibit at the Los Angeles County Museum of Art.

To my editors, readers, friends, colleagues, publishers, and family—I could not continue without you. This book is for my late brother, John Pell Bitting.

COVER ART

"Dummy Ventriloquist" by the inimitable artist & writer, Emmet Abrams

ABOUT THE AUTHOR

Michelle Bitting was short-listed for the 2023 CRAFT Character Sketch Challenge, the 2020 Montreal International Poetry Prize, the 2021 Fish Poetry Contest judged by Billy Collins, and a finalist for the 2021 Coniston Prize. She won the 2018 Fischer Poetry Prize, Quarter After Eight's 2018 Robert J. DeMott Short Prose Contest and is the author of five poetry collections, *Good Friday Kiss*, winner of the inaugural De Novo First Book Award; *Notes to the Beloved*, which won the Sacramento Poetry Center Book Award; *The Couple Who Fell to Earth*; *Broken Kingdom*, winner of the 2018 Catamaran Poetry Prize; and *Nightmares & Miracles* (Two Sylvias Press, 2022), winner of the Wilder Prize and recipient of a starred review and Best of Indie 2022 from Kirkus Reviews. She was a finalist for the 2020 Reed Magazine Edwin Markham Prize, as well as the 2021 Ruminate Magazine, 2019 Sonora Review and New Millennium Flash Prose contests. Other credits include the Beyond Baroque and Glimmer Train poetry awards and finalist for the Poets & Writers Magazine California Exchange, the Rona Jaffe Foundation, the Julia Peterkin, and Rita Dove poetry awards. Poems have been nominated for Pushcart and Best of the Net prizes, as well as Nimrod's Pablo Neruda, American Literary Review, and Tupelo Quarterly's Poetry Awards. Michelle is a Senior Lecturer in Poetry and Creative Writing at Loyola Marymount University and Film Studies at U of Arizona Global.

MICHELLE BITTING

C&R PRESS CHAPBOOKS

C&R Press hosts two chapbook selection periods from June to September and November to March each year. The Summer Tide Pool and Winter Soup Bowl Chapbook Series are open to new and established writers in poetry, fiction, essay and other creative writing genres.

2023 SUMMER TIDE POOL
The Consolation of Geometry by Alice Campbell Romano

2023 WINTER SOUP BOWL
Allison A. deFreese's translation from Spanish
of Luciana Jazmín-Coronado's *Dinner at Las Heras*

2022 SUMMER TIDE POOL
The Ice Beneath the Earth by Brian Ascalon Roley

2022 WINTER SOUP BOWL
tommy noun by Maurya Kerr

2021 SUMMER TIDE POOL
Rocketflower by Matthew Meade

2021 WINTER SOUP BOWL
We Face the Tremenedous Meat on the Teppan
by Naoko Fujimoto

2020 WINTER SOUP BOWL
My Roberto Clemente by Rick Hilles

2019 SUMMER TIDE POOL
Inside the Orb of an Oracle by Dannie Ruth

2019 WINTER SOUP BOWL
The Magical Negro Reveals His Secret by Gabriel Green

2018 SUMMER TIDE POOL
Yell by Sarah Sousa

2018 WINTER SOUP BOWL
Paleotemptestology by Bertha Crombet

White Boys from Hell by Jeffrey Skinner

2017 SUMMER TIDE POOL
Atypical Cells of Undetermined Significance by Brenna Womer

2017 WINTER SOUP BOWL
Heredity and Other Inventions by Sharona Muir

On Inaccuracy by Joe Manning

2016 SUMMER TIDE POOL
Cuntstruck by Kate Northrop

Relief Map by Erin M. Bertram

Love Undefined by Jonathan Katz

2016 WINTER SOUP BOWL
Notes from the Negro Side of the Moon by Earl Braggs

A Hunger Called Music: A Verse History in Black Music
by Meredith Nnoka